LITTLEWOODS POOLS GIRLS

JOAN BOYCE

Writing on the Wall
Toxteth Library
Windsor Street, Liverpool
L8 1XF

Published by Writing on the Wall, 2021

Photographs from Littlewoods Log Archive
& Littlewoods From Peace To War

Layout & Design by Katrina Paterson

ISBN: 978-1-910580-42-4

0151 703 0020
info@writingonthewall.org.uk
www.writingonthewall.org.uk

Stay up to date with our latest books, projects, courses, and events with our newsletter. Sign up on our website
writingonthewall.org.uk

CONTENTS

Foreword

I first got to know Joan when she and her husband Frank took part in a Writing on the Wall project celebrating the life and work of seaman, writer, playwright and social activist George Garrett. Joan mentioned to me that she had written a book about Littlewoods, based on interviews with the women who had worked there, but was having difficulty getting it published.

I immediately thought of another famous Liverpool firm, Tate and Lyles, which my mother worked for from the age of fourteen until she turned thirty, when she left to start our family. My mother became one of their youngest ever supervisors and loved her job so much that it is a standing joke in our family about never mentioning Tate and Lyle, as it immediately sets her off in raptures about working there. Even now, with the onset of dementia, her time there is something she always remembers.

The women in Joan's interviews remind me of my mother. Littlewoods and Tate and Lyle, along with some other big companies in Liverpool, were renowned for their paternalistic attitude to their employees, the majority of whom were women, although most of the managers and directors were men. For women like Joan and those she interviewed, their ability to work represented a kind of freedom, giving them a chance to earn their own money and offering a certain independence, which in turn gave their families much needed support.

Many studies and books about Littlewoods concentrate on the Moores Brothers or the economic development and impact of the company on the wider economy. Joan has done a real and unique service in her work by giving a voice to the women themselves, allowing them in their own words to reflect on their working lives and the wider social events, circles and friendships they enjoyed within Littlewoods.

Writing on the Wall are grateful to Joan for choosing us to bring her work to the wider public, and proud that we have been able to help Joan honour her promise to the women she interviewed that she would one day publish this book.

Time moves on, but it seems fitting as the iconic Littlewoods building on Edge Lane is repurposed for film studios, that the voices of the women who worked there has been preserved by Joan for future generations. It is a vital addition to the history of Littlewoods, and most of all, a tribute to the women who worked there. Joan deserves a huge amount of credit for her commitment to giving them the voice they deserve.

MIKE MORRIS, CO-DIRECTOR, WRITING ON THE WALL

Introduction

For forty years until the 1990s, Littlewoods Pools was one of the most famous brands in Britain. Millions played the Pools every week, filling in their coupon and returning it to Littlewoods. On Saturday afternoons, half the country would listen intently to the football scores on the radio to check if their coupon was a winner. The big winners were featured in newspaper headlines – and even TV plays.

Processing the millions of coupons returned to Littlewoods needed a small army of checkers - women who worked behind the scenes, without whom there would have been no Pools. This book is the story of the women that worked in 'the Pools' in Liverpool. It is also the story of the company itself and the man, John Moores, who launched the Pools from a small office in Church Street in 1926 with just £150.

In Liverpool, almost every woman either worked in the Pools or had a mother, aunt or sister who worked there. The Pools provided regular stable employment for women in a city blighted by casual work and unemployment, where women's work tended to be irregular, dirty, unsafe or demeaning.

LIVERPOOL AND THE POOLS

Liverpool was a port city. Its economy, while generating an incredible amount of wealth, had always been overly dependent on the port and its associated trades. From as far back as the 1890s this was a source of regular comment. The Liverpool Review remarked: 'We are not a great manufacturing centre. By the side of Manchester, Leeds, Birmingham, Bradford and smaller places, we have, as manufacturers, to hide our heads.'[1]

This is not to say that there wasn't any manufacturing or service sector developing. While it is estimated that in 1914 there were 60,000 workers directly employed by the docks, thousands more were employed in moving and storing goods – as carters and drivers, in grain and sugar silos, in warehouses, in cleaning and making the bags and sacks used to pack the goods.

There were thousands more in waterfront industries – tarpaulin and sail making, rope manufacturing, chandlers, paint makers and many others.

There were also industries involved in processing the raw materials that came in through the port – sugar from the Caribbean in the huge Tate and Lyle Factory, wood from the Baltic processed by match factories and bobbin manufacturers, wheat

1. Liverpool Review 26 July 1890

milled into flour, rubber into cables and tyres.

What all these industries had in common was their connection with the port – either directly or indirectly.

Liverpool's economy generated great wealth for some, but it generated exceptional poverty for many. Work in and around the docks was casual and irregular – sometimes there was no work and at other times working weeks of 60 hours or more. Pay was always low and irregular. This wealth and poverty lived side by side. The Wellington Rooms, Liverpool's premier club for the super rich, was next door to Brownlow Hill workhouse, one of the largest workhouses in Britain, with up to 6,000 paupers confined within its walls.

It wasn't until the 1920/30s that industries independent of the port began to develop. Fords opened its car plant in 1930. At the same time, The Automatic Telephone Company (the future Plesseys) started mass producing electrical and telephone equipment. But it was a question of too little, too late. While the new consumer industries were developing in the midlands and the south, Liverpool remained very dependent on ships and shipping – and the declining Lancashire cotton trade in particular.

WORK FOR WOMEN

While there was employment for women in the dockside industries such as rope making, it was often dirty and dangerous with poor pay and long but not guaranteed hours. Five per cent of working women worked sorting and mending jute bags. 'After a few hours at this work, the women became chocked with grain and mineral dust and their cloths swarm with weevils and similar insects'.[2] Work in laundries involved long hours and low pay. In 1914, 6,000 women laundry workers had had to go on strike to achieve even a 55-hour working week – and in particular, a Saturday night off.

The shortage of work and the great inequality meant that many women were forced to work as domestic servants – either living in or as day servants. In 1911, around 40% of women were working as providers of personal services (such as domestic servants, cleaners, laundry workers) including 22% of working women working as indoor domestic servants. The shortage of regular work meant many more women were forced into domestic service than in similar port cities like Glasgow and London.[3]

By the 1930s other forms of work were slowly

2. Daily Worker 1930
3. See Women workers and the sexual division of Labour in Liverpool by Linda May Grant, P 141

developing – in shops and as clerks and typists in offices, but there were not enough decent jobs for women. It was out of this world that the Littlewoods Pools company emerged. The work in the Pools was clean. The conditions were relatively good. The hours were, in today's jargon, family friendly – including a summer break at the end of the football season for looking after the kids in the school holidays or getting a temporary job at the seaside.

For 50 years, thousands and thousands of women worked in the Pools. Most Liverpool families have a relative that worked in the Pools – many until they retired. Often they would be joined by sisters and daughters. Their steady, regular work was essential to the family income in a city cursed with casual work and unemployment. The women also gained a measure of confidence and independence.

This is not to say that conditions were idyllic. In fact there was much to argue over and consequently in the 1960s, the Pools women organised themselves into a union, Usdaw, and through the union got themselves a more equal say in how things were run – as well as equal pay with the relatively few men who worked on the shop floor.

As the containerisation led to a rundown of the docks, and the 1980s economic recession hit Liverpool, these jobs became even more important to women on Merseyside and their families.

THE BEGINNING OF THE END

The Thatcher recession of the 1980s was devastating for Liverpool. The older industries associated with the port were already struggling with the decline of the docks. The newer 'white goods' industries and the car plants, branches of companies with their head offices in London or Detroit, went to the wall one by one as the recession bit.

Littlewoods Pools, with its head office and its loyalties in Liverpool, managed to work on through the recession. Its major Merseyside sites – in its iconic building in Edge Lane, in Walton Hall Avenue and in Birkenhead – all continued to function fully. As redundancies and closures took place around them, it seemed the 2,500 jobs of the mainly women workers were safe and recession proof. The women's wages ,which for years had provided them with a measure of independence, now provided welcome relief in families devastated by the rising tide of unemployment.

But Littlewoods Pools was not to survive. The economic down turn and the government's economic policies had broken so many companies on Merseyside - but they hadn't broken Littlewoods

Pools. Its end was brought about by a specific act of legislative assassination.

THE LOTTERY AND ITS IMPACT

The Conservatives manifesto for the April 1992 election contained promises to cut taxes and by extension this meant cutting public services. As a fig leaf to cover these cuts the manifesto included a proposal to introduce a national lottery to raise funds for 'good causes'. The Conservatives won the election and within a month the new government announced its intention to legislate to bring in its national lottery.

Both Littlewoods, the Pools workers and their union Usdaw, knew the difficulties that would lie ahead. The introduction of national lotteries had destroyed the Pools industries in Greece, Australia and Belgium. There was only so much money people could use for gambling and the Lottery's gain would be the football Pools loss; there wouldn't be a level playing field between the lottery and the Pools. The government proposed that the lottery would be able to advertise on television – something the Pools had never been allowed to do.

Littlewoods and Usdaw, together with the other smaller Pools companies (Vernon's and Zetters), set up a joint committee to co-ordinate efforts to try to persuade the government and MPs of the damage the lottery would do – the destruction of the Pools industry in its current form, the potential loss of 6,500 jobs across the country with very few jobs being created by the lottery. They hoped to stop the Bill or at least secure a level playing field for the Pools.

The Pools workers and their elected union reps (70 in Merseyside alone) went into overdrive. Lobbying MPs, writing to the press, travelling to London, etc., to persuade the government or Parliament to block the Lottery Bill. Usdaw provided campaign materials including briefings for members on lobbying MPs, arranging meetings with MPs and writing to the local press. One MP credited the Pools women with changing his mind. He was going to support the lottery to raise money for the NHS, but he announced in Parliament that while he hadn't been persuaded by the efforts of the Pools directors and their PR team, he had finally been persuaded to change his mind by the efforts of the union reps themselves.

Despite all the efforts of the Pools women, the union reps and the companies themselves the Lotteries act passed through Parliament and received the Royal assent on the 16th July, 1993. The fate of

Littlewoods Pools was settled.

TV advertising and roll over prizes – both unlawful for the Pools – hyped up the lottery. Then came a second weekly draw. There was a dramatic fall in the number of Pools players as people switched from the Pools to the Lottery.

As soon as the Lottery came into view, in September 1992, the Usdaw reps had had the foresight to negotiate a redeployment and redundancy agreement. The Pools women were redeployed or received some compensation for their redundancy. The union then tried to hold the line that there could be no compulsory redundancies. But there was no stopping the closure programme as the number of Pools players dwindled.

First to close, November 1994, was Liverpool's Edge Lane site with the loss of 800 jobs; ten months later, in August 1995, it was the turn of Cardiff with a loss of 330 jobs; six months later, it was the turn of Glasgow to close with the loss of 330 jobs. Then it was Birkenhead's turn. By May 1997, four years after the Bill had received the royal assent, the coupon returns had dropped 50% and the Pools industry had shrunk from 4,138 workers spread on five sites to just 1,000 workers. Finally came the closure of Walton Hall Avenue and Littlewood's sale of the Pools to a company called Sportech.

OUT OF THE ASHES

Despite everything, the Pools industry still survives in Liverpool. No longer called Littlewoods – and very different from the original Pools, there are still 250,000 regular players whose coupons are now processed by 100 staff. It survives as an echo of the 20th century institution which had households up and down the country checking their coupons on a Saturday evening as the football results were announced.

Meanwhile the Edge Lane Pools building remains as a landmark on one of the entrance ways to Liverpool. For a time it lay empty and semi derelict. Then in 2018 it was announced it was to be developed as a creative and film making hub – with a film studio complex and sound stages. It is to become 'the Hollywood of the North' - a flag ship for the creative industries that are one of the keys to Liverpool's future. While being a part of the new economy of Liverpool, it is to be called The Littlewoods Studios as a homage to the old occupants of the building.

Joan Boyce has done us all a great service with her valuable contribution to the history of Littlewoods by giving a voice to some of the many thousands of women who passed through there;

what they have to say will resonate among families across Liverpool, Merseyside and The North West, for we were all affected by their work, and the impact of the rise and fall of the Littlewoods empire.

KATHY DAVIES
FORMER USDAW SENIOR REP AND BRANCH SECRETARY AT LITTLEWOODS POOLS BRANCH.

JAMES REES
FORMER USDAW EDUCATION OFFICER.

My Days as a 'Littlewoods Girl'

I left school in 1950 when I was 15. I had no academic qualifications or any idea of what I wanted to do with my newfound freedom. Some of my friends went to work in the local factories like the British American Tobacco Company and Tate and Lyles Sugar Factory, mainly because other members of their families were already employed there.

I decided I wanted to work for Littlewoods because I already had three sisters employed in the Pools. Marie had worked in the Pools for quite a while and had worked her way up to the position of supervisor at Walton Hall Avenue. Nancy and Josie both worked in Irlam Road. All three seemed to be happy enough at their work this convinced me to do the same.

I chose to go for an interview at the Irlam Road branch. I thought I would feel more secure being with my sisters. Also, Irlam Road building was very convenient and on a direct bus route. I passed the interview and the exam and was told I could start work the following Monday. I was thrilled that I had got over the first hurdle and was soon to be a wage earner. Later, my younger sister Pat joined us. It was rapidly becoming a family firm.

My first post was as a junior in the wage office.

I felt quite important at first walking the full length of the pool room, which was larger than a football pitch, just to deliver messages or letters to various departments. I didn't learn much and there didn't seem to be much chance of getting any further in that type of work.

To me, working as a Pools clerk seemed much more exciting and interesting. The variety of jobs throughout the working week was much more appealing than delivering letters and doing errands.

The first chance I got I asked if I could be transferred to work on the Pools. My supervisor, Miss Vernon, encouraged me to remain in the wage office and give myself more time. I didn't take her advice, and arrangements were made for me to move to the Pools a few weeks later.

After a couple of weeks, I was sent down to the supervisor in charge of group L.11, a Miss Flanagan. She was a kind, caring women and she re-assured me that there was nothing to worry about, that in a couple of weeks I would be as adept at the job as the rest of the clerks. Miss Flanagan sat me next to a woman quite close to her desk where she could keep an eye on me. She explained to the women that I was a trainee and she was to give me tasks to do and in general to show me the ropes. She was to check my work and to make sure I was doing everything correct.

After two or three weeks I would be given a small position and be expected to be able to cope alone. My work would no longer be checked, I would be held responsible for any errors made, and then be considered a fully trained Pools clerk.

I soon became quite skilled at the work and enjoyed it. There were so many different tasks to cope with that you never had time to become bored. I continued working as a Pools clerk for five years, then the opportunity came for me to do further training as a typist.

I was sent to the typing school, training to become a correspondence clerk. I think I attended the typing course for about a month. It was a very intensive course. We typed all day long to music to achieve a steady pace and to gain rhythm. The keys on the typewriter were blank so we had to memorise where the various letters were, this was known as touch typing. Throughout the day we were constantly examined to improve our accuracy and build up our speed. This method of learning continued until we reached the target of complete accuracy and a speed of sixty words a minute.

I found this rather gruelling but very fulfilling. I had been given the opportunity to learn another valuable skill which has served me well throughout

my life. I worked on Corres, (short for correspondence) for the following four years. I was married in
1958, and a year later I left to have my first child.

I look back with great pleasure to the time I
worked for Littlewoods. I learned a great deal and
made many lasting friendships. I have often won-
dered if other women enjoyed working in the Pools
and had similar opinions as myself. I decided to
try and find out. That is the reason for me writing
this book.

LITTLEWOODS POOLS GIRLS

A Brief History of The Moores Family

Liverpool was a most fortunate city to have had the Moores family (Littlewoods Pools millionaires) as residents. Liverpool would have been so much the poorer without their generosity, as well as the cultural, social and artistic contributions made possible by their keen involvement in the city. What made them even more special was that, unlike many other millionaires who made their fortunes in this city, they stayed and never even contemplated moving to more prosperous destinations. John Moores was once asked why he had never moved south, nearer to London, his response was

> I have made money out of this area and I like the people here.[4]

The family were not originally from Liverpool, they first lived in Droylesden near Manchester. John moved to Liverpool when he first became serious about starting his Pools venture.

I have always greatly admired the family, but even more so since I have learned more of their family history. It was both a shock and surprise

---

4. Clegg Barbara, The Man Who Made Littlewoods. The Story of John Moores, P 26

to me to discover their humble beginnings. Their family background was not unlike many of their employees. It never entered my head when I was working in the Pools that my millionaire boss came from a very similar background to myself. It brought a smile to my face when I discovered that they entertained each other in their family parties and get togethers in a similar way to my own family. Everyone in the family played their part by performing their favourite piece, like singing their special song, or reciting a monologue or poem and even doing a step dance. Life was sweet and uncomplicated.

John Moores was one of eight children. He had three brothers and four sisters. They were a poor Lancashire family. Their father John William Moores was a bricklayer and his mother Louisa Fethney was a Mill worker, who was bright, thrifty and intelligent. John and Louisa were strict parents and like so many parents of their time always gave the boys more freedom than the girls, who were expected to help with all the household chores and general cleaning. They also had to take a lot of responsibility for the younger members of the family, nursing them to sleep and putting them to bed. All very similar to young girls who lived in my area.

The older children had jobs and gave their earnings to their Mum to help with the rest of the family expenses. When John was twelve he had a part-time job delivering milk and gave all his wages to his Mother. John was always aware of the struggles of family life and tried to help his mother and lighten her burden as much as he could.

John left school at the age of fourteen and first worked in the Post Office as a messenger boy, but he had a disagreement with one of his colleagues and left. He quickly got another job in the Commercial Cable Company as a trainee telegraphist. This move was a blessing in disguise because there were much better prospects of promotion and it paid better wages. Later John was sent to the Cable Companies training school in Bixteth Street Liverpool. It is strange to think that many years later in this very street John Moores became the owner of Liverpool Boxing Stadium. Little did he realise that Liverpool would eventually become his home and the centre of his business empire.

John attended night school learning telegraphy and at the same time did a correspondence course for the Civil Service. He was an intelligent and ambitious young man with a good head for business. Louisa, John's mother, was aware of these qualities, and fostered them in the best way she could by providing him with the space and encouragement he needed. Louisa always pointed out to him that the secret of success was to work hard and always do your best.

On January 26th 1917, John wrote a very moving letter to his mother to thank her for her good wishes on his 21st birthday. He wrote,

> Dear Mam, thanks so much for all your good wishes. Knowing how sincere they are I value them beyond measure. I value them and view them not only as wishes (though that were enough) but as tokens of faith and confidence that I will make good. Standing, as I do, on the brink of Manhood and my career, and facing the world, they are doubly cheering. They comfort me, they inspire me, strengthen me. And seem to bring to the top all that is good in me. Can I but keep them then I shall prosper; and can I but keep them, life will have been well lived - and worth living. Give me them, then, now and always, and whatever success I shall have, yours will be the bigger share in it. I say success, and with all due gravity and confidence; not because I am strong enough to command circumstances, but because I feel

that with such wishes supporting me, I
must and will succeed, in so far as good
for me.[5]

I'm sure his mother must have kept this letter for
the rest of her life. All her advice was obviously
being taken seriously. John seemed determined to
make good because of her faith in him. Most of us
try our best and work hard to achieve our aims, but
do not have the success of John Moores. It takes
more than ambition and luck to rise from poverty
and obscurity to gain such great wealth and power
as he did. John was without doubt a clever person
with very special talents and gifts. We learn more
about the man and his character from other peoples'
comments and the effect he had on their lives.

John's father had been ailing for a very long
time and consequently out of work. The family were
constantly short of money. John's mother worked
very hard to keep the family solvent. At one point
she took in sewing, but that did not pay well, and
then tried her hand at opening a sweet shop, but
that didn't make any money and she found herself
even more in debt.

Louisa had to borrow money from her sisters to
pay off her debts. The family moved house to make
a fresh start and Louisa opened a chip shop. When

5. Ibid, P 11, 12

times became too difficult she even had to resort to secretly pawning her husband's pocket watch. She always had to make sure that she could redeem it before the weekend in time for him to attend church.

John's father died of tuberculosis in 1919. It was at this point that John took it upon himself to become head of the family and vowed that he would look after his mother and all the family. John was very close to his mother and was always conscious of her struggles. He never forgot her advice that the secret of success was to work hard and to always do your best. John worked hard throughout his life, and, when possible, he involved every member of the family in all his ventures.

For the rest of his life he continually felt responsible for the care and welfare of his mother and the rest of the family. From what we now know, it is obvious that John had inherited his mother's energy and perseverance of constantly being one step ahead with new ideas to make money, so that the family could enjoy a decent living. John's mother was lucky to have lived long enough to share and enjoy his success.

The Start of the Littlewoods Football Pools

Early in the 1920s John was now working for The Waterville Cable Station in County Kerry, a branch of the Cable Company in Liverpool. This was a time of swift progress and great importance of international trade and communications. As soon as John had learned to read cable slips and achieved the skill of total accuracy in touch typing, gaining an impressive speed of seventy words a minute, he was posted to Ireland. The role of The Waterville Cable Company was to receive messages from the Americas and re-transmit them to Liverpool and London.

John lived in a large community centre along with 150 other workers, and shared a bedroom with a friend called Colin Askham. Colin had been a friend of John for many years. They had both been Post Office messenger boys in Manchester and had spent a lot of their spare time together, playing golf and engaging in long conversations about what they intended to do when they returned home.

Money was still a big problem in the Moores household. John felt obliged to send most of his wages home to his mother to keep the family afloat; he also managed to save money by doing overtime and getting involved in other money-making ventures.

The food in the community centre was of poor quality, so John formed a committee to try and improve things. Using his own savings, John set up a small company called the Waterville Supply Company. Instead of ordering the food from local firms who were charging over the odds for inferior goods, he ordered all the food direct from Dublin and England at a lower cost. This made life more pleasant for everyone, as well as making a profit for himself.

Likewise, John negotiated a similar deal with Dunlop's. There was no sport shop for miles around, so he offered his services to become an agent for golf requisites, mainly to supply golf balls. In this instance he gained twice; he got golf balls for his own use and made 30% profit on all his sales. At the end of eighteen months when he returned to his old job in Liverpool, John had saved a thousand pounds.

Not long after returning to Liverpool, John and Colin met up with another old friend, Bill Hughes. Bill had also been a Post Office messenger boy in Manchester. The three of them spent a lot of time together after work and spent many long hours discussing ways of how to achieve their ambitions to make money.

John had read about a man called John Jervis Barnard who lived in Birmingham and had tried to run a football pool, but his efforts had failed. John was intrigued and couldn't wait to find out more information about this man. Bill Hughes offered to make enquiries and managed to find out more information and secured one of Barnard's coupons. Barnard had based his pool on the French betting system, which was that 10% of the total stakes would be subtracted for management costs with the rest divided among the winners.

The three friends spent a great deal of their spare time mulling over Barnard's ideas trying to work out how many coupons he would have had to print and distribute before making a profit. The whole thing became an obsession. It was not long before they decided that they could develop their ideas further and make things work.

So far, all their discussions and ideas about setting themselves up in business had been in their spare time and in private. There was a very strict rule in the Cable Company that no outside employment was allowed. If any employee was found setting up other business interests outside, they would be sacked on the spot.

Neither John nor his two friends were in a financial position to allow this to happen. In theory they all agreed with the rule, but they didn't think their enterprise would interfere with their loyalty to the firm. Their main worry was to keep it a secret and to keep their jobs. To do this they had to come up with another name to use.

Colin's parents had died when he was a baby and he had been brought up by an aunt and later adopted her name. He had originally been born Colin Henry Littlewood. They all agreed that it would be a great idea to use Colin's birth name. Their new venture would be named 'Littlewoods Pools.' They knew that this was going to be a costly venture, and after a great deal of serious thought and discussion they each decided to put up £50 to start it off.

The following day they met at the bank. All three were feeling very anxious but at the same time excited about their new project. John describes his feelings.

> As I signed my own cheque, my hands were damp. It seemed so much money to be risking.[6]

It's hard to believe that the multi-million-pound Littlewoods Pools empire was built on a £50 shared

---

6. Ibid P, 30

idea all those years ago. Determination, faith and most certainly genius, must have been at the root of this success.

The Pools venture had a very shaky start, and was not by any means an instant success. After the initial decision of the shared enterprise, the next step was to find premises. A small room was rented on the top floor of an office block, 38 Church Street, in the centre of Liverpool. The rent for the room was 25 shillings a week. The next expense incurred was 30 shillings a week for a typist.

The football season had already started, and they still didn't have a printer to print the coupons. Bill managed to find one in Duke Street, a Mr. Bottomes, who promised to do them a fairly cheap deal, and printed 4,000 coupons as a start.

It seems rather a naive idea to us now, nevertheless, John took himself up to Manchester United's football ground and organised a group of young boys to go around the ground and distribute the coupons. John was afraid to do this himself in case of being seen by any one from the Cable Company, resulting in his instant dismissal.

> I hovered on the fringe of the crowd,
> torn between the desire to supervise
> this haphazard operation, and fearful

of being seen by any official of the Commercial Cable Company.[7]

This was the first step on a long arduous journey to success.

John had to be even more vigilant because he was now married to Ruby.

The result of that first marketing experience was very disappointing. Out of the 4,000 coupons distributed only 35 were returned, bringing in a total of £4.7.6d. The first dividend was £2.12s, added to this was the 10% they had agreed on to cover their expenses. Left with a deficit, the partners each had to put more money into the kitty. Not to be put off, they were determined to try again. A further 10,000 coupons were printed and distributed at one of the big matches in Hull.

Only one was returned.

The situation didn't improve, and so the partners had to continue putting more money in, without any returns. It was all getting to be too much. Bill called an emergency meeting; he was very worried and wasn't sure what to do next. After much discussion he said,

Let's face it ...we've lost nearly £600

7. Ibid, P 30

between us. It sounded like a good idea,
but obviously it will never work. I vote
we cut our losses and drop the whole
thing.[8]

Colin agreed with Bill and they both waited in
anticipation for John's response. With very little
hesitation he said,

> I'll pay you back what you've lost so far
> - that's £200 each - if you'll sell me your
> shares in it.... I still believe in the idea[9]

I suspect that this must have been one of the most
regrettable financial decisions that Colin and Bill
ever made.

John had always been used to being his own
man and making all his own decisions. Now he was
in a different position, this was such a big risk and it
was only right that he consulted Ruby his wife. Ruby
listened intently and they discussed their finances.
Things would be very tight, but she encouraged him
to follow his instincts and go ahead with his plans.

> If you don't, she said, you will never
> quite convince yourself that another few

8. Ibid, P 32.
9. Ibid, P 32.

months might not have turned the tide.
I'd sooner be the wife of a man who has
gone broke than a man who is haunted
by regret.[10]

There were long difficult times ahead. The office in
Church Street had to be cancelled. The whole family
came together to help. All the work of distributing
and marking was carried out from John's home in
Walton, but despite all their efforts, John was still
losing money.

When John went to pay his printing bill Mr Bottomes suggested that he should change from the
French system of taking 10% for expenses, to taking
all his expenses for printing, stamps and stationery,
plus a small commission. John couldn't believe that
he hadn't thought of this solution himself, it seemed
so obvious. He put the idea into practice and things
immidiately started to improve. The receipts at the
end of the 1926 football season were £258, a vast
improvement. Brighter days to come, not only for
the Moores family but also for Liverpool.

The Pools went from strength to strength and
soon there was far too much work for the family to
cope with alone. The time had finally come for John
to leave his post in the Commercial Cable Company
and devote all his time and energy to working full

10. Ibid, P 33.

time in the family business. New premises were rented, again in Church Street, but this time on the top floor over a cafe called King's Cafe. John's sisters Hilda, Lou and Edna, as well as his brother Cecil, now also worked full time in the new office.

John decided to advertise for young school leavers offering them work. He took on about 10 boys and at this point just a couple of girls. Many years later two of these boys became directors in the firm. By coincidence they both had the same surname, Jackson, so from then on, they were referred to as 'Red' and 'Black' Jackson, because of the colour of their hair, a simple solution.

However, success was short lived and blighted by an oncoming court case. The police brought a prosecution order against the firm for contravening the Ready Money Betting Act. Apparently, there was a phrase in the act that said,

> It is an offence to make payment on or
> for a bet to be determined thereafter[11]

According to the police the whole business of betting on the football Pools was illegal, even to print coupons was against the law.

John and Cecil had to attend the hearing at the magistrate's court and to their great dismay were

11. Ibid, P 38.

convicted. The situation seemed to be insurmountable but John, not to be defeated, immediately lodged an appeal. The appeal was granted, with the second hearing of the case due to be heard at the following quarter sessions.

By this time the case had attracted a great deal of public interest. The details were covered in the press and Littlewoods was rapidly becoming a household name.

The recorder examined all the fine details of the case and decided to uphold the appeal on a technicality. It appears the impossible had happened. The brothers had won their case, but most of all they had gained so much free publicity. Once again, things had worked in their favour.

The popularity of the Pools increased beyond all expectations. By March 1927, over 20,000 coupons were being received on a regular weekly basis and the takings had increased to over £2,000. The following season this increased further to 50,000 coupons and takings of £4,000 per week. The profits were ploughed back into the business and they moved to larger premises in 44 Whitechapel. The football Pools were here to stay.

Success continued, but there had already been several instances of punters trying their hand at cheating. Immediate action had to be taken to prevent further attempts. John and Cecil put their heads together and tried to create a foolproof security system to prevent further fraudulent coupons from being smuggled in along with the legitimate ones.

The first move was to have all the mail delivered straight to the Post Office. There, every envelope would be franked with a special franking machine devised by Cecil. This machine would punch pin holes straight through the envelope and all its contents giving date, time and registration. When all this had been done, the sealed sacks would be collected by staff members of Littlewoods.

The Moores brothers had the ability and knowledge to develop ingenious methods and ideas like this new franking machine and would always be one step ahead like the astute businessmen they were.

At weekends, when the football results were coming in, half the country would be glued to the radio checking their coupons hoping for a win. Staff were often asked to work overtime. They didn't mind staying back because they knew that their efforts were appreciated, and of course they would be paid well.

Money was always a great incentive for the workforce, but it was in everyone's best interest to pull together and maintain the firm's continued success. This was done very much in the spirit of teamwork. The family worked alongside the workers and continued working long after everyone else had gone home. They never expected anyone to do anything they were not prepared to do themselves.

It is obvious that the success of the football Pools cannot only be attributed to the genius of John Moores and his family but also to his very loyal workforce. John Moores himself would be the first to admit this overtime was taken on board willingly for the boss they greatly admired. The mutual respect they had for each other is confirmed in the following comments.

> He was a man who inspired loyalty. The whole family did. We called them the royal family....we used to refer to them like that.[12]

John always referred to his female workers as 'my girls'.

> We got to the stage years later that we were rather elderly girls, but he still called us 'girls.' 'He was an excellent man to work for.[13]

12. Ibid, P 46
13. Ibid, P 46

It is difficult to comprehend that the popularity of the Pools continued and increased despite the imminent and famous world slump and the Wall Street crash of 1929.

The whole world was experiencing an economic crisis which sent unemployment to great heights. Merseyside suffered more than most. All the service industries which it totally depended on, like commerce, the docks, the railways, and shipping were all in deep decline, with one in three local workers out of work.[14]

Despite prosperity being at its lowest and unemployment at its highest, Littlewoods Pools were recruiting more and more staff each week, while other firms were laying them off. At this point, Littlewoods were providing jobs for over 10,000 people, the majority of whom were women, which was a great help in reducing the dole queues.

Many families were experiencing extreme poverty. One can only deduce that the increase in people trying their luck at the football Pools was an attempt to try and win money as a means of personal survival.

> During the between-war years the football Pools did more than any one thing to make life bearable for the

14. Caradog Jones, Vol. 11, P 336.

unemployed...[15]

Business was booming, with profit for the 1929/30 season reaching over £19,000. By 1931 it had increased to nearly £47,000, and by the 1934/35 season, takings had reached the colossal sum of £200,000. The Moores family were now extremely rich. Their success prompted many other competitors across the country - Vernon's Pools Liverpool, Soccer Pools Leicester, Zetter Pools London, Empire Pool Blackpool, but none of this competition affected Littlewoods, in fact it was probably beneficial for the industry as a whole.

The speedy expansion of the Pools required more and more premises. Buildings were acquired all over the city, 34 Pall Mall, Brownlow Hill, Hood Street, Williamson Street, Leeds Street, and Walton Hall Avenue. Later, Walton Hall Avenue premises became the headquarters. By this time the firm had begun to diversify into horse racing and printing. The beautiful Art Deco building in Edge Lane was purpose built to provide even larger Pools space as well as very large premises next door to accommodate J&C Moores print works.

The newfound wealth affected the private lives of the whole family. John was the first to move to a modest four bedroomed house in Victoria Road,

15. Quote from George Orwell... Displayed in Preston Museum.

Freshfield. The house was named 'Fairways'. Fresh-field is a quiet residential area north of the city. Later, he bought a second house for his Mother, this was quite close to his own in Larkhill Lane. Over the following few years the whole family had followed suit and all settled nearby.

Cecil and his wife Doris lived in the same road as John. Lou and her husband Len had a large detached house built close to Cecil. Hilda and George were a little more adventurous. and bought a large house in nearby Birkdale, which is closer to the larger town of Southport. It is hard to believe, but all this was happening during the years of the depression when most of the country was in turmoil. The Moores family were at last reaping their hard-earned rewards.

There was none more surprised at their success than John Moores himself and his family at the speed and enormous success of the Pools business. Here was John at the tender age of thirty-five and already a millionaire. John began to wonder whether the success had anything to do with good organisational skills and business sense or whether it was just a fluke. John confided in Cecil about his doubts and asked him

Cecil, do you think we've been rather

lucky? Was it all a fluke? If we'd gone
into any other sort of business, d'you
think we'd have done as well?[16]

John had to prove to himself that more than luck
was necessary to succeed in business, and started to
make enquiries into the mail order business. John
was always conscious of the financial problems
experienced by large working-class families, having
been there himself. This kind of enterprise could
be a two-edged sword. If it became a success, John
would prove to himself that he had good business
skills, make even more money for himself and his
family, as well as helping poorer families to provide
for their children.

In 1932, just before John's thirty-sixth birthday,
Littlewoods diversified even further, and Littlewoods Mail Order Stores was born. John passed all
the responsibility for the football Pools over to Cecil,
but always kept a watchful eye in the background.
John put all his time and energy into concentrating
on his new challenge. Like the Pools, there was lots
of hard work and struggle ahead, but success in the
Mail Order business was achieved much sooner.

By 1936, just four years in the making, mail
order returns totaled over £4 million a year. John
had proved to himself that luck was not the only

16. The Man Who Made Littlewoods. The Story of John Moores, P 52

factor in achieving success; he had made his second million and he was a very happy contented man.

The well-established empire of Littlewoods was not only interested in furthering their business success but also in finding ways of rewarding their workers. They were always fully aware that without a dedicated and loyal workforce none of their success was achievable. The Moores brothers firmly believed that a happy appreciated workforce always produced the desired results.

By 1939, Littlewoods was to face the biggest problem that any businessman could ever imagine. England was in serious danger of another war. A couple of weeks later on the 3rd of September, the whole country listened to Neville Chamberlain's speech; England was at war with Germany.

One might imagine that this massive upheaval could mean the end of the Littlewoods empire. No such thing. In August the previous year, when John and his family had been holidaying in Scotland, he had received a telegram from the Government saying that in the event of a war they may have to purchase all the blankets he had in his warehouse. Within two days, all Littlewoods stock had been dispatched to Whitehall. Later, John and Cecil offered all their premises and available staff to the Government to assist in the war effort.

WORLD WAR TWO

At the start of the war two buildings were immidiately taken over by the Government. One was the new purpose-built Art Deco Pools building in Edge Lane. It was equipped with extra telephones and desks for His Majesty's Censorship Department. Incidentally, the agreement made was that all the buildings were at the Government's disposal for the duration of the war. Littlewoods did not gain access to the Edge Lane building for ten years after.

The second building was Hanover Street, which was fitted out with sewing machines in preparation for the production of parachutes. Several groups of Pools clerks had been taught by experts to cut, sew and assemble parachutes. Staff were moved into the building and proceeded to carry out production. Later, Hanover Street became one of the leading parachutes centres in the country.

Canning Street, Birkenhead, became the next centre to be taken over to produce Barrage Balloons. Making balloons proved to be a very difficult business. Groups of women were taught by experts at the Dunlop's factory. It was messy and precision was essential. It involved a process of sticking, sewing and taping all the different pieces together. There were many teething troubles to start with but eventually things were sorted, and the workers became adept at the job.

The only way the company could cope with production demands was to have a continual assembly line. This meant organising three shifts. John took it upon himself to make sure that things ran smoothly ,and moved a bunk bed into his office and slept there on site. After the night shift left, John would help to clean and tidy up the place and prepare it before the day shift arrived.

He even started night classes to help the girls to perfect their work by practicing on spare pieces of material, such was the determination of the man to ensure perfection from his workers and to make everyone's contributions, efficient and safe.

All the finished balloons were then moved to a building in Irlam Road, Bootle to be assembled and tested for faults before being exported to their final destination.

Little did I realise that all this important and difficult work had been performed by ordinary women who had first been employed as Pools clerks. They had had no previous experience in this field before, but did the work admirably and with outstanding success. To think that all this took place in the same building that I, as a naive fifteen year old, would eventually work as a Pools clerk, years later.

By 1944, over sixteen buildings had been taken over by the Government. They had all been fully equipped and furnished with all the necessary materials required for jobs taken in hand. Over 14,000 workers were employed.

The results of the overall achievements of staff and workers was:

- From March 1940 to September 1945, 5,080,000 Parachutes.
- From September 1940 to December 1944, 20,411 Balloons.
- From June 1942 to March 1945, 11,756,000 Shells.
- From June 1943 to June 1945, 735...Wellington Frames.
- From March 1942 to June 1945, 6,068,000 Fuzes.
- From December 1942 to October 1945, 4,534 Pontoons and Storm Boats.
- From March 1941 to June 1945, 49,589 Dinghies.
- From September 1942 to November 1945, 24,298 Annual Production of Boxing.[17]

This magnificent achievement was not plain sailing. During the famous May Blitz of 1941, some of the buildings, while in full flow of production had direct hits causing complete destruction and several fatalities.

17. From Peace to War. A record of Littlewoods Wartime Achievements. (Liverpool Records Office), P 286-288

Buildings were swiftly vacated, and alternative premises had to be found and set up to enable work to continue. It is remarkable that such a feat was carried out and achieved with such outstanding results, especially as the workers had had no previous experience in this type of work.

John and Cecil Moores were often overcome with surprise at the resilience and adaptability of their workforce. Many were young and keen and always pulled their weight. It never ceased to surprise the brothers how quickly they learned and mastered new, intricate tasks.

This only proved to John, what he had always believed, that given opportunity, good guidance and encouragement, most ordinary people can learn and master new and unfamiliar skills in a short space of time and carry them out with efficiency. It would appear from the results of the work produced, that once again he was right.

The two brothers and their workforce were not the only ones who put their backs into the war effort. The rest of the Moores family members also did their bit. Having the good fortune to own large houses in the suburbs, they opened their doors and took in Liverpool evacuees who were victims of the May blitz. Their large gardens were turned over to rearing pigs and poultry with the flower beds used to grow vegetables.

These arrangements played a major part in helping the family to provide good food for everyone concerned and to enable them to cope with the new enforced rationing. Lou converted the local village hall into a canteen for soldiers who were billeted in a nearby barracks. Ruby, like many other local women, became a valued helper in Formby's W.V.S. (Women's Voluntary Service).

At the end of the war both John and Cecil made the following announcements to state their pride and pleasure for their war-time achievements.

It is indeed a source of great personal pride and pleasure to devote my endeavor and resources to the War Effort. If the Company was successful in its war time undertakings that is my reward. In so far as our combined efforts have helped to shorten the war, that is due to the industry, honesty of purpose, will and co-operation of all those - executives and staff - who supported Mr. Cecil Moores and myself in overcoming every difficulty. - John Moores.[18]

That Mr. John Moores, myself and the

18. From Peace to War. A Record of Littlewoods War-Time Achievements, P 7

organization of Littlewoods were able to play an integral part in furthering the cause of Great Britain, her Empire and her Allies is a fact for which I am profoundly grateful. I feel honoured that our earnestness received such sympathy from the government, and support from each and every one of our workers. That I was fortunate to be one of such a grand team was an immeasurable reward in itself. - Cecil Moores.[19]

19. From Peace to War. A Record of Littlewoods War-Time Achievements, P 9

Watching a performance during lunch break

Working on the Pools coupons

Supervising

Sorting

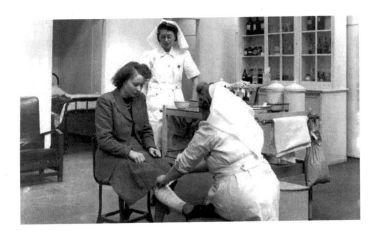

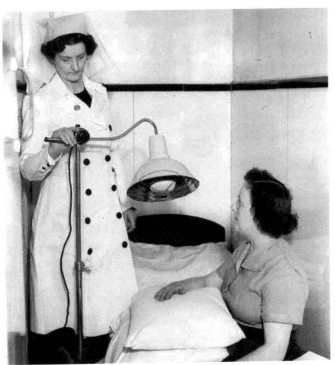

Workers receiving treatment at a nursing station in the factory

Old Hall Street, Head Office of Littlewoods Mail Order Stores Ltd

Edge Lane, Head Office of Littlewoods Pools

The Canning Street Building in 1939.

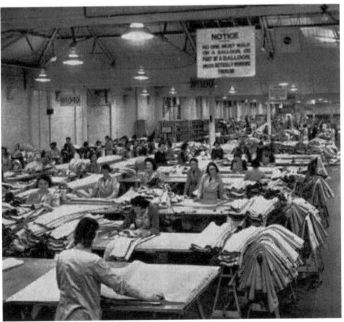

The same building in 1940 making balloons

The Walton Hall Building in 1939

The same building in 1940 on War Work

The Irlam Road Building in 1939

A section of the same building in 1942 making Pontoons

THE LITTLEWOOD

REVIEW

ol. 2 No. 1.   Issued by H. LITTLEWOOD Ltd.

The company magazine The Littlewood Review reported on company business and staff events...

...a day out at Blackpool...

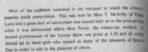

...sports days...

...swimming galas....

...and Littlewoods Girls' having fun at the Pleasure Beach

On the road - fleet of buses carrying Littlewoods workers to Blackpool

Littlewoods building today

John Moores in the 1940s

Photograph of sculpture by Tom Murphy, photographer: Rodhullandemu

Bronze statue of John & Cecil Moores, founders of Littlewoods Football
Pools, in Church Street, Liverpool

PEACE AT LAST

The end of the war, which had wreaked such devastation, also brought great joy and happiness, as families were re-united with fathers, brothers and sisters returning from the armed forces to enjoy family life again. Although there was a great sense of relief and optimism, there were also feelings of fear and worry about how to cope with all the devastation and lack of amenities.

There were difficult times ahead, not only for the general public but also for the business world. Many firms had fallen by the wayside and disappeared altogether; others were struggling to re-establish themselves. Littlewoods had played a very successful part in the war effort, but like everyone else it had to now face up to the difficult task of rebuilding their own business enterprises.

Many of their buildings, offices and shops had been either damaged or completely destroyed. Immediate plans had to be put into action to get things replaced or put back into working order, to allow them to switch back from being munition factories to being shops, offices and pool rooms again. Each section of the business had their own problems to contend with. As well as sorting out premises there were many other drawbacks.

At the start of the war the Government had requested the three major Pools firms, Littlewoods, Vernon's and Zetter Pools, join forces and become Unity Pools.

Unfortunately, the Board of Trade did not allocate them any paper. To overcome this problem, they advertised their coupons in some of the daily newspapers.

The first obstacle The Pools had to face up to was another court action. A clergyman accused Unity Pools of breaking a clause in the Betting and Lottery Act. This stated that publishing coupons in the press was breaking the law. The clergyman won his case. The Pools could not continue to use the newspapers to print their coupons. This really did seem to be the last straw and the end of the football Pools.

The Government intervened and said that it was through serious and unforeseen circumstances as well as the outbreak of the war that had forced the Pools to have to resort to using the press to print their coupons. In the present circumstances, it was now time to reconsider their situation, to allow them to stay in business. To resolve the problem, the Government decided to allow them a limited supply to read: paper. This they believed would enable them to print their own coupons.

Although the coupons had to be drastically

reduced in size, the company was once again out of danger.

John, never slow on the uptake, fully understood that the Government's intervention had nothing to do with allowing them to get their businesses back on the road again. John knew it was more likely to make sure that they would not lose out on receiving large amounts of money in taxes and other revenues which the company generated. His response to this move was,

> They must have decided that they valued the millions of pounds we paid in income tax, postage stamps, duties, etc., apart from the fact that we were employing more than 10,000 girls in a depressed area and putting employment stamps on their cards.[20]

The first hurdle for the Pools was successfully remedied with the paper allowance. Then a few months later, Unity Pools closed down. Each of the firms involved went back to building up their own business. This had a favourable effect for Littlewoods; very soon they were back to where they had left off and once again became the biggest Pools firm

20. The Man Who Made Littlewoods. The Story of John Moores, B. Clegg, P 120.

in the country.

For the Mail Order and Retail areas of the firm, things were not so simple. They had to face up to far more serious problems, like clothes rationing and finding new suppliers and, in many cases, new premises. The added drawback of paper shortage was another problem.

Paper was a real necessity for the Mail Order division and the shops to get started again. It was needed to produce catalogues and advertising. There was also the added problem of parceling goods for dispatch. Coping with all these major setbacks meant that it took much longer for these areas of the business to get back on track.

On a more serious note, John's policy of ensuring jobs for all those employees returning from the services was proving to be virtually impossible. Many of them had been employed in the Mail Order and Retail section of the business. and they were still struggling to get things up and running. At that point in time there really weren't any jobs available

The only solution the brothers could come up with to keep their word and ensure that all their former employees had a job was to transfer many of them over to the Pools section of the company, where more workers were required. Most people just wanted a job, so they accepted the situation and adjusted to the work involved.

Because of the continued popularity of the Pools, Littlewoods recruited more and more workers. More buildings were being acquired all over the city. The system was that as new buildings were found, workers living within a five-mile radius would be transferred to it. This system seemed to suit the workers; it wasn't daunting in any way because you knew all the girls that would be moving with you and travelled together every day.

Littlewoods was growing so fast it was rapidly becoming an empire. It was wonderful for Liverpool's economy. Thousands were employed, not only in the Pools but in all the firm's other enterprises. Littlewoods employed the largest number of women of any commercial company in the country. This had a twofold effect. Every Thursday when all the Pools women had a day off, Liverpool's city centre would be packed with them spending their hard-earned cash, which was very good for the economy. Anyone will tell you it was always easy to spot a Littlewoods girl, they were always dressed in the most up to date fashions long before anyone else.

Having said that, many men were also employed by the firm. Nearly all the top jobs in the Pools, such as executive posts and directors, were staffed by men. Then there was the security, staffed by ex-policemen, detective sergeants and inspectors. There was also a great army of maintenance workers, electricians, mechanics, painters and decorators, plumbers and joiners. As well as making the firm totally self-sufficient, it provided many men with good, steady, well paid jobs, another plus for the city.

The fact that most of the top jobs were staffed by men seems rather unfair considering that the vast majority of the workforce were women. It is good to know that, later, this policy did change, and many women eventually held executive posts too.

Voices of the Women

It is interesting to note that only three of my interviewees had worked for Littlewoods before the war, the rest were new to the firm

Mary Hill was one of the three who started working for Littlewoods in 1940. Mary was too young for the Armed Forces but was eligible for war work, and so worked in the Canning Street building making parachutes. As a young girl she said:

> It didn't register with me at the time how important the work was. I remember having great fun and lots of laughter with all the other women. We got ourselves into a mess many times, but it all turned out fine in the end.

Mary now looks back on that time in her life with great pride.

Marie Bigley, a 15year old, started her new job in 1943. Marie was too young for military service and war work, but she got a job as a Pools clerk. Being totally new to the firm she recalls working as a young trainee in the Hood Street building still used for the football Pools. Marie explains how they received flimsy coupons that had been cut out of the newspaper. Some of them would be in a poor state and scruffy. This made them a bit difficult to deal with. They first had to sort the coupons into alphabetical order, then mark them to see if there were any lucky winners.

> I found it a bit tedious sorting them out, but it was exciting and interesting work, very different to school. I felt grown up that I was now a wage earner. I didn't feel stressed in any way about making mistakes, because I knew my work would be re-checked.

Margaret Brown started work in 1942, like Marie, she was employed as a Pools clerk. She was also based in the Hood Street building. She said:

> I was frightened to death at first, but everyone was so helpful and kind I soon got the hang of things and managed fine.

All three women remained working for the firm for many years.

Out of all the thirty-three people that I interviewed or who completed my questionnaire only one person, Anne Baker, said that they didn't enjoy working for Littlewoods Pools. She said:

> You had to have speed. I felt under pressure all the time. No matter how fast I worked it was never fast enough. The women were always kind and helpful, but I couldn't keep up. I stuck it for two years, then I'd had enough, I gave up.

Although everyone else said that they enjoyed the work, they all admitted that there was an element of both fear and pressure on you most of the time, but you learned to take it all in your stride. Most workers eventually managed to learn and build up their speed. But a lot of the time you were in fear and trembling of missing client's winning lines when marking the coupons. These were referred to as 'extra winners'. If you were guilty of this too many times you were in serious trouble. You were sent to the head supervisor of your department and put on a warning. If it happened too many times you could end up being dismissed.

I don't have any idea of how many women this may have happened to. The fact that no one referred to any such occasion makes me think it was rare. That is not to say that it never did happen. Several of the women did mention being sent to Personnel and being reprimanded. Miss Profitt, the Personnel Officer, would try and find out if you had any personal problems that she could help with before putting you on a final warning. She also sent for you when you had been late several times or absent without a doctor's note and gave you a good telling off.

According to all my interviewees, Littlewoods was an excellent firm to work for. They paid higher wages than most other employers in Liverpool. Mr. John and Mr. Cecil were always fair minded and showed great interest in their workforce and appreciation for loyalty and good work by setting up various schemes of encouragement and bonus systems.

Marie Bigley said:

> I loved every minute of my time working in Littlewoods. They were wonderful people to work for kind and considerate and they also paid good wages.

Clare Halford also said:

> Littlewoods was a very good firm to work for. It was a family firm really concerned about their staff. Mr Cecil

was an excellent figurehead, often visible on the shop floor, stopping and chatting asking how things were and how you were coping, or if you had any problems. You always felt that these enquiries were genuine and that they wanted a contented happy workforce.

Josie Stubbs said:

Littlewoods were a very good firm to work for. The employees were always treated very fair. It was a family firm and they did so much for Liverpool. In my opinion they did not get the recognition they deserved earlier.

Norma White pointed out:

Although Littlewoods was a large firm everyone seemed to know each other. Everyone got on well with each other. There was always a good caring atmosphere. The Personnel department seemed to know everyone as an individual. It was a family firm rather than a large corporation. It wasn't unusual to see one of the directors stop their car and pick you up if you were waiting at a bus stop. This kind of thing made you feel you were just as important and appreciated as those in the top jobs.

Anne Brennan had similar views as the others. She said:

Littlewoods were a fair and considerate firm. In the early days we were not unionised but as far as I was aware most people felt that we didn't really need to be in a union; we were treated fine without one. We had a staff council elected by the workers. They met on a regular basis and were always available for the women to put forward any grievances, worries or problems they had. At the meetings these were always fully discussed and sorted. It suited us and it worked very well. In later years when the firm grew very large, we did become part of USDAW.

The firm's policy of giving workers the opportunity to improve and to gain promotion was another plus. They believed that it made good sense to give everyone the opportunity to contribute not only to the development of the firm but also to develop personal talents and abilities to the full. In this way everyone would benefit.

Workers were always given the chance to train for other jobs. When higher paid positions became available, the policy was to promote from within instead of bringing people in from outside the firm.

As Marie Bigley pointed out:

> We were educated by the Moores family, they didn't bring outsiders in to fill higher paid jobs, they trained us, and gave us the chance to improve and benefit both academically and financially.

She was right, John and Cecil Moores didn't only provide opportunity for their workers to train in other fields and gain promotion, they also sponsored large numbers of employees to follow courses in Further and Higher education.

Evidence of this can be found in the firm's monthly staff newspaper, the 'Review', where every month photographs of successful candidates were shown being congratulated on gaining Open University degrees and other academic qualifications.

Once again this demonstrates their keen interest in individuals wanting to broaden their horizons.

The popularity of Littlewoods as a good firm to work for was not only judged on the fact that the pay was better than most, but also on the many other facilities made available by the management for their workers.

The welfare department in every building was of a very high standard. Two qualified nurses were always on hand to deal with any minor ailments. Doctors were on call to deal with more serious situations.

As Marie Collins noted:

> This provision was available to all the workers long before the introduction of the N.H.S. (National Health Service.).

As early as 1937 Littlewoods also produced a pension scheme for their employees. One director said,

> A marvelous thing at that time, and it was certainly unusual then.[21]

The Moores brothers were always thinking ahead to provide the best for their staff.

If a person was absent from work for more than

21. Ibid, P 81

a fortnight the health visitor would call on them, firstly to bring them their sick benefit but also to see if they needed any extra help. When they eventually returned to work they were offered the opportunity of taking a holiday in Glentrool Scotland to convalesce. This was a shooting lodge owned by the Moores family. When the family were not using the house they made it available to all their workers whenever they wished to take advantage.

The main purpose of this offer was to provide respite, or for women to convalesce after being ill. Occasionally it would be used as a reward for good work or just for a well-earned holiday Everything was laid on free of charge, including transport to and from the house as well as board and food.

Anne Brennan recalls the time when she was given the chance to go to Glentrool for a holiday:

At the time I was from a poor working-class family and had never been away or any further than the Pier Head. It was a magical time for me. During the day we were taken around all the sights in a Minibus. In the evening after a wonderful dinner we would go to the games room and play table tennis, cards or have a dance. We had the time of our lives. They were such generous people, millionaires who were prepared to share their wealth with so many others.

Angela Moran, who had worked her way up to a very important high-status job, explained to me that the after care of employees was crucial to the firm. Mr. John and Mr. Cecil strongly believed that every employee's contribution was equal in importance for the smooth running of the firm, a cog in the wheel you might say. Mr. John was a hard a task master, strict and tough, but he was always fair and considerate; he demanded respect, honesty and loyalty. These were his own principals and he fully lived up to them. He was an example to us all. Angela shared this very moving and emotional story concerning a cleaning lady.

> This woman was a very conscientious worker, never late or absent, totally reliable. One day she was absent. She sent in the usual doctor's note. When the health visitor went to visit her to bring her pay, she was appalled at her living conditions. Later the lady was admitted to hospital seriously ill.

Whilst in hospital the Company arranged to have her outstanding utility bills paid and her home made more comfortable. Curtains, bedding and food were provided.

> When she returned home, she was delighted with her new home. Unfortunately, her pleasure was short lived, and she died very shortly after.

The Moores did their best to try and locate some of her relatives or friends but the search proved to be fruitless. They immediately set to and organised the arrangements for her burial.

Not only did they organise and pay for her funeral but they made sure that a number of the staff were present to give her a good send off.

This was not a one-off situation, there were many more like it, but they were carried out unobtrusively. This was typical of the care and attention that Mr. John and Mr. Cecil gave to loyal staff. They never made any fuss, they just got on with things. Very few people knew about such events. The Moores brothers just thought it was right and proper to acknowledge loyalty.

How many large firms today would treat their workers with such respect? Littlewoods was a very large firm employing over 30,000 staff in Merseyside alone, not to mention those employed in Glasgow and Cardiff. It is a great credit to them for their outstanding humanity. Most large firms have no idea of who their staff are or what they even look like, for them they are a mere faceless number on their payroll.

The firm was also at the forefront of promoting other health programmes. Every year they arranged for mobile ex-ray units to visit all their buildings to test for TB (tuberculosis), and breast cancer, as well as the blood donor service. Regular eye tests were encouraged and visits from the chiropodist to treat tired or damaged feet. All these facilities were provided for everyone who wanted to take advantage of them. They were also carried out on the spot during working hours to make things more accessible and to encourage workers to look after their health.

The working environment always seemed to be in a state of improvement. The presence of the maintenance staff was continually visible, painting and repairing, and generally making the surroundings more pleasant and cheerful.

Although the pool rooms were very large, accommodating hundreds of working women, they were bright and airy to work in, sufficiently warm in the winter and pleasantly cool in the summer. This was fine for the majority of workers, but not for a couple of women who worked in one of the smaller offices who strongly disagreed

Norma White was a secretary to one of the managers. She worked in a small office just off the Pools room. This is what she had to say.

> Our office had a glass roof; it was very cold in the Winter and blazing hot in the Summer. We used to make ourselves paper hats out of newspapers to shield our heads from the heat......we must have looked right nutters wearing our hats while answering the phone and typing our reports, but we were desperate, we needed to demonstrate our dilemma. Our efforts were duly noticed. Eventually things were sorted out and we were able to carry on with our work without our hats.

ORDER OF THE WORKING WEEK

A Pools clerk's work was very varied, you never had time to get bored. Every day was different. Monday you could hear a pin drop. Every head was bent and in deep concentration marking the coupons and extracting winners. You had to give this task your complete attention, but at the same time not lag behind.

For some, for fear of missing a winning coupon, this was a nerve-racking job. Many women were really fast at this job, but they were always willing and helpful to those who were not so adept. By the end of the day you felt totally drained and ready for home.

Tuesday was paying-out day. Clients winning small dividends were dealt with by the Pools clerk responsible for that particular client's entry. Larger winners were dealt with in a different department called Central Registers and Central Claims.

Josie Stubbs, who worked in this department explained:

> I worked in Central Registers, where we dealt with ready cash. We were constantly under surveillance by security. At first this was rather intimidating, but

you got used to it. The security staff were quite friendly and you realised they were just doing their job.

Central Claims was where we typed out the cheques for big winners. You had to take your time and make sure you didn't make any errors. The completed cheques were taken to the accountant to be checked and sent out to the client. We were terrified of him. He always seemed to be serious and unfriendly.

One day, one of the girls took her cheques in to the accountant. We heard him shouting and really telling her off. She was sent back to re-do some of her cheques because she had spelt 'forty' incorrectly, adding a 'u' spelling it 'fourty'; they had to be destroyed.

She was so upset, and it didn't help her confidence one bit. We all thought she was treated a bit harshly, it was quite an easy mistake to make. We didn't much like the accountant after that. '

In the afternoon the Pools clerk's job was to enter the client's account with the amount of his stake. This was referred to as 'entering'. The amount of the postal order received was checked with the amount the client had gambled. This was then entered on to his personal plate. It was a slow and tedious job, but it was easy and didn't cause any anxiety.

Wednesday, in stark contrast, was so noisy it was like experiencing the bombing in the war again. It was 'running off' day, addressing the envelopes to send out the following week's coupons to the clients. Everyone would raise themselves up by sitting on their PO (postal order) box. This was believed to give more force when embossing the envelope with the client's address. This was achieved by placing the clients metal plate into the addressagraph, known as the 'Joey', and giving it a mighty strike. The noise was incredible, and your arms would be nearly dropping off, but it produced the desired results and as soon as the exercise was finished the happier everyone was.

The rest of the day was different again, filling the envelopes with a coupon, a copy coupon and any other information that the management felt they wanted to include. The first thing to do was to stamp all the coupons with your own position number. This was a sight to behold. The women would fan out the coupons and proceed to stamp them in the tiny square provided. The precision and speed they worked at was incredible. Then, using a rubber thumb, they would pick up each item and thrust them into the envelope with such speed and agility that it was much quicker and swifter to observe than any machine.

The workers performed these tasks to the sound of piped music, often singing along to the song being played. This created a very happy atmosphere. The singing was very effective because the movements of the hands seem to synchronize with the beat of the music that was being played.

Some of the more cynical women suggested that the idea of playing piped music had an ulterior motive and was a deliberate ploy on the part of the management. They believed that as time went on the management increased the speed of the music to make the women work faster. Whether this is true or not we will never know.

Thursday was a day off, and probably for most the happiest day of the week. After a good break and a sleep in, many would make their way into the city shopping centre to spend their hard-earned cash and to meet up with friends This, at the same time, would be a great help to boost Liverpool's economy.

Friday was back to the grind again bright and early. The whole day was spent opening the post containing the current week's coupons. Anne Brennan recalls her days as a slitter:

There were forty-eight women on a group.
At the end of each group there were a

set of pigeonholes containing a space for each person on the group. My job as a slitter was to sort the mail into these pigeonholes according to the number on each envelope. To help to speed things up the women formed a rota system, two at a time came to assist me with the sorting.

When the pigeonholes were full, I would take the post out and slit the top of the envelope on the slitting machine. I would then take them to the clerk for opening. Slitting the top of the envelope helped the women greatly. It gave them a start to open the rest of the envelope with much more speed and made it easier for them to extract the contents. I liked this job very much, the women were always praising me for being so quick and attentive; they often treated me to a cake for my break.

Every item received had to be stamped with the plate in the 'Joey' containing that week's code. This was an extra security precaution to prevent fraudulent coupons somehow entering the chain. It was another noisy day but in retrospect quite varied and interesting.

Often a coupon would arrive in an envelope containing your position number but would not belong to your position. The clerk receiving it would try to locate the correct position. She would say, 'Pass that to Barnard Castle, or pass that to Hexham or some other place, just words really, I had no idea where these places were.'

Now, years later travelling around the country by car, I often spot signposts with some of these name places on them. It brings a smile to my face and evokes happy memories of my days working.in the Pools.

Saturday was a repeat of Friday, opening post for most of the day. When that job was complete silence would descend while everyone concentrated on sorting the coupons into alphabetical order and stringing them into manageable bundles for easy marking on Monday morning.

Opening post involved so many different tasks you never noticed the time passing. It seemed that no sooner had you arrived in the morning that it was time to pack up and go home and look forward to the week-end break. This was the pattern of events followed week by week.

Of course, by the early sixties, long after I had left, everything changed dramatically. The introduction of new technology meant that a lot of the work was done by processing machines, computers and scanners. All the jobs previously done manually were mastered in half the time. For all this speed to be achieved, staff had to be trained to use these machines and learn all the new skills.

Everyone was entitled to two week's holidays with pay every year. This increased according to the length of an individual's service. Similarly, sick pay allowance was two weeks per annum. If you didn't need to use up your sick points, they were carried over to use the following year.

Littlewoods company was also a member of Employers for Childcare, they made sure that maternity, paternity and adoption leave was made available to all employees.

The canteen provisions were excellent too, very good food at subsidised prices. Most people took advantage of the opportunity to make good use of it, not only for the good food but to relax and have time to be with friends. Nearly every lunch hour entertainment was provided either by your own building's concert party or from a visiting one.

The talent was amazing, with dancing and singing as well as funny comedians. You had such a good laugh and it really set you up and refreshed you to carry on with your work in the afternoon.

SHORT TIME

At the end of the English football season there was a changeover to Australian football. There wasn't the same amount of interest; fewer people filled in the coupons so most of the workforce went on short time. You could either work three days and be paid for four, work four days and be paid for four and a half or work five and be paid for five.

The majority chose to work the three days. Some had their usual Thursday off but then got other work, waitressing or working as shop assistants.

Margaret Smithwick explained:

> When the football season ended, we were all left with time on our hands. because we went on short time. I chose to work the three days. I got a job as a waitress in Southport from Friday through to Sunday. It was really hard work but a huge change from the Pools. I went with two other girls. We got the train from Exchange Street Station, still in use in those days. It went straight through to Southport, which was very handy. I have lots of happy memories so it couldn't have been that much of a

chore, but I found Pools work far more enjoyable.

Some left the firm for the whole of the summer season to spread their wings in pastures new. Many went to work in Butlins or Pontins holiday camps, a totally different experience to working in the Pools. But when the football season started again, they all returned to their old jobs, with lots of exciting tales to tell.

Many really relished this set up. It gave them the opportunity to have a complete change and to experience different types of work. For some who worked in the holiday camps it was a great adventure and the very first time they had been away from home.

Lily Jones recalls:

> I went to work in Butlins, Pwllheli North Wales, with a friend. We were so excited, we thought we were going on a long holiday. What a shock! We worked very long hours with very little time to enjoy ourselves. The work was hard, boring and repetitive, not a bit like what we had expected. We were disappointed, so we didn't stay very long. We returned

home and got work in T.J.Hughes department store. That wasn't too bad, but sometimes customers were difficult to deal with. I enjoyed the change and the chance to experience life away from home. It was at this point that I realised how much I enjoyed working in the Pools. I missed my friends and all the laughs we had, and I looked forward to returning to work when the football season started again.

Sports and Entertainment

Littlewoods didn't only give space and time for workers entertainment during working hours, they also provided a network of sports and social clubs, for after work activities. These facilities covered a wide spectrum to cater for most interests. They included competitive team games, like netball, rounders, tug of war, ladies' football and running.

Each building was encouraged to form their own teams. Every year a sports day was organised where teams would compete. There was a lot of rivalry but all in good fun. The sports days were always a great success and well attended. Most of the worker's families attended too. Special events were set up for the children to take part

Then there was the arts and crafts section where people entered their work in the competition. These covered subjects like landscape and portrait paintings, photography, dressmaking, knitting, crochet work, embroidery, tapestry work and soft toy making. Some of the work was so beautiful and professionally carried out it must have posed a very difficult job for the judges.

One of the highlights every year was the 'Miss Littlewood' competition. It was always a very exciting time. Many women were encouraged to enter the competition by their colleagues and management. Each building would have several entrants. All the rest of the workers in each building would vote for the person they thought should win. The lucky winner of each building would gain the title of that building and go forward for the final. The overall winner of all the building's finalists would be the new 'Miss Littlewood' for that year.

Norah Horrigan, a Pools clerk in Irlam Road, Bootle, remembers being summoned to the manager's office.

> I was just seventeen at the time Mr. Woods the manager of our building sent for me. I was shaking like a leaf. He was a bit like a sergeant major, very stern. He told me that my friends had put my name forward to enter the 'Miss Littlewood' contest. I was both shocked but at the same time relieved because I thought I had done something seriously wrong. I strongly refused to enter saying that I was much too shy and not good enough. He tried his best to make me change my mind, but I wouldn't budge. Anyone who knew Mr. Woods would find this hard to believe he was such a hard,

tough man, but he was very gentle and kind to me. I left his office and floated down the stairs feeling wonderful and flattered, but I never did enter the competition. I missed my chance.

Every month each employer would receive a copy of the Littlewoods Pools staff newspaper, 'The Review'. This paper would give all the news of what was happening in each building, information like who was getting married, who was engaged, who was retiring as well as lots of other interesting and helpful hints and important events.

A month or so before the 'Miss Littlewood' competition was to take place a voting slip was included plus a photograph of all the buildings' finalists. Every employee had the opportunity of making their personal choice of who they thought should win the title.

The wheels would then be set in motion for the arrangements of the Big Night. Over the years these took place in a few different venues. The early ones took place in the Liverpool Stadium, which sadly no longer exists. Others were held in The State Ballroom, Dale Street, some held in the Liverpool Empire Theatre.

It didn't seem to matter which venue was used,

it was always a splendid occasion. The main spectacle of the evening obviously centered around the election of the new 'Miss Littlewood', but there were lots of other items of entertainment too.

Many famous celebrities and stars were included in the programme.

Josie Stubbs remembers Tom Jones the singer performing and Jack Jackson the famous trumpeter Anne Brennan remembers Donald O'Connor doing a dance routine and Maureen Maddock remembers Cliff Richards being top of the bill.

This information was printed in a copy of the 'Review' before one of the competitions:

> Months of preparation will culminate in a sparkling show of shows at the Empire Theatre, Liverpool. Cliff Richard will top the bill and no doubt the rafters will ring with cheers and applause. Then, in the final few minutes a voice will echo around the theatre with these words, 'Miss Littlewood 1980 is...' 'So, who will it be?[22]

Maureen Maddock says:

> I was lucky to see the last Empire Theatre

22. Littlewoods Review, Issue 58

show which included Cliff Richard and Cannon and Ball. It was absolutely fabulous and a night to remember, but like everything else things change.

The final 'Miss Littlewood' competition was held in 1992. The competition had been going for forty-seven years, but it was felt that it was time for a change. The competition was replaced by a new event called 'Achiever of the Year'. Some were sad to see it go, others felt it was out of place and didn't fit in too well with the new ideas of what the role of women were, and the views of the then active Women's Liberation Movement who were against the exploitation of women.

MEMORABLE DAYS OUT

Littlewoods organised many social events for their workers. The largest and most difficult to arrange was the annual trip to Blackpool. The trip to Blackpool was arranged every year as a treat before the commencement of each Football season. In 1939, just before the outbreak of the Second World War, the largest ever organised outing by any firm in Great Britain was arranged by Littlewoods for all their employees.

On this particular year it had to be planned and carried out over two days to accommodate the large numbers. Each day 200 coaches set out from various parts of the city to rendezvous on the Ormskirk Road, Liverpool, where the convoy was to be formed. The fleet of coaches was so large that special arrangements had to be made with the police. Traffic lights were regulated to prevent any major hold ups. 12,000 people including Directors, Chief Executives and all the rest of the workers travelled together to enjoy this exceptional excursion.

What a magnificent achievement. It is hard to imagine how such a spectacular event could ever have been even attempted. Imagine this happening today, even on our so-called streamlined roads and motorways. There would be total chaos and massive holdups.

Every one of my interviewees talked about these day trips with great relish. Margaret Smethwick says:

> The trips to Blackpool were wonderful, Mr. John and Mr. Cecil accompanied us on these occasions, they joined in all the fun and frivolity with such ease. The grand finale on one of these days was a firework display, the first I had ever seen. The display ended with images of Mr. John's and Mr. Cecil's faces illuminating the sky. I was mesmerised, I had never seen anything so wonderful. I still remember it, so it must have made a deep impression!

On several occasions the destination changed to Llandudno, or The Lake District, and a couple of times the firm chartered a boat to The Isle of Man, but the favourite place seemed to be Blackpool.

THE FAMOUS CHOIR

Many people will know about the 'Littlewoods Girls' Choir' or the 'Littlewoods Songsters'. Every building had its own choir but if members wished they could audition for the central choir. This choir was trained by professional voice experts. They were also given dance lessons by the famous Liverpool choreographer, Sheila Elliot-Clarke.

Being a member of this choir was a full-time job. They trained in the central club rooms in Dale Street every day from 10.a.m. until 4.p.m. All their costumes and shoes were paid for by the firm. They performed on Radio, Television and the Theatre. The main objective for forming the central choir was to raise money for orphaned and disabled children of Merseyside.

Eventually the choir was taken over by George Mitchell and later amalgamated with the 'Black and White Minstrel Show' It was at this point that other women were recruited who had no connections with Littlewoods. Littlewoods pulled out and gave the members the option of returning to their old jobs or remaining with the choir.

Maureen Richards was one person who stayed with the choir, tells her story:

I had two and a half years touring Australia and New Zealand, later returning to do two years at 'The Victoria Palace' London, and then several Summer seasons at Morecambe. I doubt Mr. John could have foreseen the career some of us would follow. It is with great thanks to him for all the invaluable training we received while being part of Littlewoods firm. Littlewoods certainly shaped our future lives.

It is commendable that a person would want to say a special thank you and to pay such an honest tribute to a former employer, to show her gratitude to him for giving her the opportunity and excellent training to follow a new career.

John's own 'motto' came to fruition in this instance, it was 'Opportunity Made, Not Found'.

Rewards for Long Service

So many of the women remained working in Littlewoods Pools for the whole of their working lives. In my sample alone, six women were rewarded for forty years' service and a further two for twenty-five. In every single copy of the 'Review' that I had the pleasure of reading, there was photo evidence showing groups of workers being rewarded for long service, receiving their cheques and special gifts from either Mr. John, Mr. Cecil or one of their sons.

When Sir John became older and more frail and he felt unable to attend these celebrations, another member of the family would replace him, but he made sure that he would be there himself to do the business if it was a member of the cleaning staff or a canteen worker. Sir John was always eager to point out that every member of staff was of equal importance in the running of a successful business.

The facts seem to speak for themselves of why so many staff remained working for the firm for such long periods, as many of the women I spoke to said, 'It was like being part of a big family.'

Littlewoods set up several clubs in the city for the over sixties and for retired employees. The idea behind this venture was to help their ex-workers to keep links with their friends. This provision surely proves the recognition they wanted to give to their loyal workforce and the paternal care they felt necessary for their continued welfare, even after they had left the firm.

I was lucky enough to attend one such group who meet every two weeks in the Adelphi Hotel. I was greatly impressed to see how many women had taken advantage of this provision. There were at least thirty women present. It was good to see so many happy people enjoying each other's company and generally benefitting from their meetings.

LIFE IN THE COMMUNITY

The Moores family's interests stretched far beyond the workplace They were deeply involved in the community at large and the culture of the city. They contributed to so many good causes to try and improve the quality of life in Liverpool.

One of their favourite charities was the annual outing to Southport for handicapped children. Many people lined the streets to see rows of motor cars and taxi's taking these children for a pleasant day out at the seaside. It must have been a wonderful feeling for the Moores seeing all those happy smiling faces leaving the city, especially as they knew that they were instrumental in making it all possible. Mr. John or Mr. Cecil usually accompanied the children on these trips.

In 1956 John Moores became the Chairman of this organisation. Later similar outings for handicapped children were organised by Littlewoods worldwide.

In the early sixties Littlewoods joined forces with Liverpool City Council in funding and building boys' clubs and youth clubs in and around the city. Edge Hill Boys' Club was the first in 1961. By 1963 there were seven more. There was always a member of the family or the firm on the management committee.

This helped to maintain stability and the professional running of the clubs.

John's eldest son, known to all as John Junior, became very active in this area. He was always interested in boxing, having been captain of the boxing team when he was a student at Eton. This stood him in good stead when later he started teaching boxing in the boys' clubs in Bootle. He was still keen and interested in the development of youth programmes until his death, aged 83, in May 2012.

The family have all been keen supporters of the arts. In 1957 John Moores sponsored the 'John Moores Liverpool Exhibition', which is held in the Walker Art Gallery every two years. The idea behind this venture is to give young up and coming artists the opportunity to display their work and to continue with their studies. The first prize in the competition is the handsome sum of £20,000, a very welcome help to any young artist. The first winner of this prize was a young David Hockney, another was the now famous Peter Blake.

The exhibition is very prominent in the art world and now an important event internationally. Some believe that it was influential in the decision to have the Tate of the North brought to Liverpool. If this is correct, this is another plus for Liverpool and the

Moores family.

Sir John has also made many generous donations to the Liverpool Playhouse Theatre and the Royal Liverpool Philharmonic Orchestra. John's other son Peter, also through his charitable foundation, brings to the city and underwrites the cost of tickets and finances opera recordings and productions sung in English.

Even before Peter set up his foundation, he personally gave help to the then virtually unknown artists Joan Sutherland, Geraint Evans and Colin Davis. Just think, we might never have had the pleasure and enjoyment of these great stars without the assistance given to them by the Moores family. Peter's foundation funds scholarships for young musicians and singers. It also continues to give its support and interest throughout the artist's careers.

Sir John had a personal interest in football for most of his adult life. In 1987 he sponsored the League Cup. In 1994 Littlewoods were the first sponsors of the F.A. Cup Competition. John became Chairperson of Everton Football Club from 1960 - 1965 and again from 1972 - 1973. He showed a deep concern for the welfare of the supporters and played a major role in improving Goodison Park, Everton's football ground.

He made an enormous contribution to football

in general on Merseyside. He had a keen interest in both senior clubs, and always believed that a certain amount of healthy competition produced good results. He was also the main sponsor of the Merseyside Youth Games.

It is a pleasing thought to know that the football mania so prominently displayed among most Liverpool people had, and still have, other staunch supporters in the Moores family and the firm of Littlewoods.

Over the years the Moores family have had to cross many bridges and drawbacks to make their business interests survive. They persevered through thick and thin and always managed to come up trumps and win their way through.

One of the biggest knock-backs the Pools had to face up to was the introduction of the National Lottery in 1994. Analysts predicted that the Pools would lose around 10% of its punters. If only this had been true. The Pools actually lost 40% in five weeks.

Littlewoods could not compete with the National Lottery's huge jackpots. One of Littlewoods largest and record-breaking payouts was £2.9 million against the Lottery's £10 million. It obviously didn't dawn on the punters that the odds of winning the Lottery were far greater than winning the Pools.

It is strange how things work out. Cecil, who at least in name (John was forever vigilant), had been in charge of the Pools section of the firm since 1932, was spared these massive changes. He died after a long illness in 1989, at 87 years of age. John would never know about the impact of the National Lottery, dying in 1993, aged 97, just one year before it was introduced. Maybe this could be considered as a kind blessing.

The year 2000 was the end of an era Littlewoods Pools was bought out by its new owners, 'Sportech' for £161 million. Since taking over they have introduced many new ideas and ways of betting. Punters can now use the internet and television to place their bets. These innovations are proving to be successful; the company is still flourishing today.

There is little doubt that Littlewoods have been a unique company. It was one of the largest privately owned firms in Europe. The Moores brothers conducted their business affairs in an extraordinary honest and humane manner. They ploughed all the profits back into the firm, not only for the benefit of their own families, but for all their employees too.

One hears these days of businesses putting profitability before the welfare and interests of their workforce. Profits seem to be syphoned off by directors and shareholders, rather than being ploughed back into the development of their business. It's doubtful if many modern businesses will follow the business ethics of John and Cecil Moores.

Likewise, the relationship between business and philanthropy has been replaced by professional fund raisers. The funding of charitable work in this country now relies more and more on organisations such as the National Lottery, Kids in Need and Red Nose Day.

My Views Confirmed

The research and writing up of my work on the Littlewoods empire has been a journey of enlightenment for me. I hope that others who may read it will enjoy it and be as impressed as I have been in discovering the extent of the Moores family's involvement in Liverpool.

The provision of employment by Littlewoods has been a major asset, particularly for women. At one time they employed over 30,000 people in Merseyside alone. Sadly, this number has greatly decreased since the closure of the stores and the Pools, and the reduction in the size of the Pools industry.

Apart from this, the artistic, cultural and leisure benefits to the city and its people are extensive. The biennial Art Exhibition and contributions to theatre, music and education surround us each day.

It is a puzzlement why it took so long for John Moores and members of his extended family to be acknowledged. Just to consider the contribution John, Cecil and their workforce made to the war effort alone, surely was commendable.

The growth to the country's economy, particularly to Merseyside cannot be ignored.

This same sentiment has been voiced by many

people before, particularly among their employees. Eventually the honors came one after the other. In 1970 Mr. John was given the Freedom of the City, in 1971 he was awarded the C.B.E. and finally, in 1980, he received a Knighthood. These honors may have been a long time coming, but worth the wait.

Looking back to the 1950s when I worked in the Pools the Littlewoods empire was still in its infancy. Even then it was a very happy place to work in. From the feedback that I have received from my questionnaires and interviews my own feelings have been confirmed. Littlewoods was a great firm to work for, they paid good wages and treated their staff with care and respect. Will we ever see the likes of them again?

The demise of the Littlewoods empire left a gap in the business world, the economy and the high street, but its impact on our history our culture and our community will remain.

Bibliography

Clegg, Barbara, *The Man Who Made Littlewoods. The Story of John Moores*. Hodder and Stoughton. 1993.

Reed, Phil, *Football and Fortunes. The Inside Story of Littlewoods Football Pools*, 1923-2003.

Author Not Listed, *From Peace to War. A Record of Littlewoods War-time Achievements*.

Members of Merseyside Socialist Research Group, *Genuinely Seeking Work*.

Mass Unemployment of Merseyside in the 1930s.

Sir John Moores Supplement to the Liverpool Echo, Thursday, January 25,1996.

Barrett, Tony, Sport Journalist Daily Post.

Notes

Responses from Thirty-Three Interviewees and Personal Interviews.

Copies of Littlewoods Staff Newspapers *The Review*.

My Research

I first approached each of my three sisters. I asked them to complete a questionnaire that I had prepared. I then did in-depth personal interviews with them. I was delighted to discover that each of them felt the same as me, and had lots of personal experiences to share.

Each of them gave me names and addresses of friends who had worked with them. They also completed my questionnaire and in turn introduced some of their friends. Things snowballed, and in the end I sent out forty-five questionnaires. I am pleased to say that thirty-three women completed and returned them to me by return of post. Four were returned to me as 'not known at this address.' The remainder didn't reply.

I tried to develop the questions on the questionnaire in a way that would give me a detailed and full overview of the women's experiences. Not only about the work itself but also about pay, working conditions, friendships, leisure activities and general feelings about the firm and its management.

Every single person who replied seemed keen and pleased to hear that I intended to write up my findings and try and have them published. Several of them allowed me to do taped interviews of their experiences.

I also managed to contact Marg Carey, a woman who worked closely with John Moores for many years, who was a union official and a member of the Union of Shop, Distributive and Allied Workers (USDAW).

I received a great deal of help from Angela Moran, a woman who had a high-profile job in Littlewoods for many years. She continued working in the Pools when it was taken over by 'Littlewoods Promotions Limited, 'Sportech'. She has been able to provide me with a great deal of information about Littlewoods and of employees who worked for the firm over recent years, as well as some women who are still employed by the new owners.

Angela kindly provided me with a copy of *From Peace to War: A Record of Littlewoods War-time Achievements*, as well as many photographs and other important historical notes.

I have also had the privilege of using Barbara Clegg's excellent biography of John Moores, *The man who made Littlewoods. The story of John Moores*, which was published in 1993, just before he died.

Tony Barrett, former sports journalist at The Liverpool Echo (currently Liverpool FC's Head of Club and Supporter Liaison), was generous in providing me with a lot of information on the Moores family and the development of the football Pools.

The contents of this work may be considered as being biased and one sided. But the method I used to collect my information was by personal interviews and by asking each candidate to complete a questionnaire. I have written up my findings as told to me. To acquire an alternative view will be an opportunity and the work of someone else.

Acknowledgements

I would like to express my sincere thanks to all who have assisted me in writing this book.

Thank you to Angela Moran, Director of Littlewoods (Sportech). Angela was the first person I contacted. She read my script with interest and introduced me to a couple of her colleagues who were really helpful.

Barbara Clegg's *The Man Who Made Littlewoods* is the only substantial work I found concerning the Moores family. I got in touch with Barbara to ask her permission to use her book, she kindly agreed.

Tony Barrett, Liverpool FC's Head of Club and Supporter Liaison, was very helpful in providing me with further information concerning the Moores business empire.

Thanks also to Marge Cary and Kathy Davies members of USDAW for their practical help.

Special place and thank to all the women who gave so much of their time and enthusiasm for taped interviews and the writing up of their memories and experiences, without them there would be no book. Namely:

Pat Atkinson, Mary Aylward, Anne Baker, Lil Beasley, Betty Bellion, Marie Bigley, Anne Brennan, Dot Bromilow, Margaret Brown, Marie Collins,

Louise Corden, Kathy Davis, Maria Dry, Geraldine Duffy, J Dykes, Maureen Galvin, Anne Grace, Clare Halford, Marie Hardwick, Mary Hill, Nora Horrigan, C. Howes, Pauline Hughes, Maureen Maddock, Joan Morrissey, Maureen Richards, Margaret Smithwick, Josie Stubbs, Marie Warburton, Betty Wilson, Norma White.

Thanks also to Professor Roger Webster of Liverpool John Moores University for his encouragement and wise guidance.

Thank you to Alexander Jackson, Collections officer and staff at the National Football Museum in Preston where the Littlewoods Archive is based.

Thank you to James Rees and Kathy Davies for an excellent detailed introduction providing important historical and business context.

Special thanks to James Moores and Kirsten Suenson-Taylor for their generosity supporting the production of this book.

I am especially grateful to my husband Frank for his unfailing encouragement, patience and humour, throughout what seemed like a life time.

Finally to Mike Morris and the team at WoW (Writing on the Wall). For their conviction and belief that the work should be published as documentary evidence and local history of a time of great hardship, unemployment, and poverty, and the changing role of women's work in Liverpool.

But most of all a tribute to the Moores family for their loyalty to Liverpool.

Afterword
Writing on the Wall

Writing on the Wall is a dynamic, Liverpool-based community organisation, founded in 2000, which delivers an annual festival and creative projects with diverse communities across the Liverpool City region. WoW celebrates writing in all its forms and works with a broad and inclusive definition of writing that embraces literature, creative writing, journalism and nonfiction, poetry, song-writing and storytelling. We work with local, national and international writers whose work provokes controversy and debate, and with all of Liverpool's communities to promote and celebrate individual and collective creativity. WoW's creative writing projects support health, wellbeing and personal development.

Joan is one of the many people we have been proud to support to tell their story.

If you have a story to tell or would like to take part in or work with WoW to develop a writing project, please get in touch – we'd love to hear from you.

Mike Morris and Madeline Heneghan, Co-Directors
info@writingonthewall.org.uk
www.writingonthewall.org.uk
0151 703 0020
@wowfest